ARE WE TOO OLD TO HOLD HANDS?

A New Beginning

ISBN: 978-1-63901-459-0 (Paperback Edition)
ISBN: 978-1-63901-460-6 (Hardcover Edition)
ISBN: 978-1-63901-458-3 (E-book Edition)

Some characters and events in this book are fictitious. Any similarity to the real persons, living or dead, is coincidental and not intended by the author.

Book Ordering Information

Phone Number: 315 288-7939 ext. 1000 or 347-901-4920
Email: info@globalsummithouse.com
Global Summit House
www.globalsummithouse.com

Printed in the United State of America

EDWARD SCHWARTZ IS THE AUTHOR
OF THE "TAPESTRY TRILOGY"

TAPESTRY

TAPESTRY TWO

TATTERED TAPESTRY

ARE WE TOO OLD TO HOLD HANDS?

It was as if we were standing on the beach and a large wave came crashing over us, leaving us naked, without fear or regrets, all having been washed over leaving two new people to restart their lives and begin again.

TABLE OF CONTENTS

Are We Too Old To Hold Hands?

A New Beginning

POETRY BY
EDWARD SCHWARTZ
Narrative by Mary Wezeman

PREFACE

*M*y name is Ed. My wife, Joan, died on April 8, 2020. It was probably the hardest thing I've ever gone through, except perhaps for my daughter's death from breast cancer in 2001. The story of my sixty years with my wife are all told in *"Tapestry"* and *"Tapestry Two."* The third book, *"Tattered Tapestry,"* summarizes our last year together. Some of the poetry is sad and some uplifting. I do hope many who have gone through this situation will, after the sadness, realize that life must go on and there is light at the end of the tunnel.

But now I am here to tell you that there is more. My wife and I had been friends with another couple. John died of cancer nine years ago and we kept in touch with Mary. I would call her once a month, more or less, to talk about my new poems, books that we had read, and music we both loved. Mary had sent us notes, birthday cards, and we exchanged books that we liked.

After Joan died, Mary and I often took walks and talked. We were two old friends who had known joy and now knew sorrow. We found we had more than sorrow to talk about because we shared so many interests.

Today everything has changed. At my age I could have been sitting in a retirement home and slowly but surely leaving this world. But instead, we are planning trips (when covid allows), reading plays together, listening to the classical and pop music we grew up with, and loving each other with a freedom we have never known. I no longer look at the calendar - just the weather forecast.

To all aging singles out there I say, "Don't give up." If you can get out of the house, lean on those friends who want to help you enjoy yourself in these last years. Who knows, one hundred, one hundred-five, maybe more. You might even bump into a new love, as I did.

You see, while we were walking and talking, neither of us saw what was coming. The last thing we expected was that friendship would turn into love. And love simply overwhelmed us. It was as if we were standing on a beach and a large wave came crashing over us, leaving us naked, without fear or regrets, all having been washed over leaving two new people to restart their lives and begin again.

CHAPTER 1

My name is Mary. I am eighty-five years old. And I have fallen in love. I am not senile, silly, simple or addlepated. Time and gravity have caused sags and wrinkles and I'm a little hard of hearing. But my mind and heart are still twenty-five. And I am truly in love, for the second and last time of my life.

This is my story.

I was married almost fifty-one years when my husband John died. I believe we had it about as good as it gets. I also think I was the envy of most of the women who knew us. I loved him; I liked him; I enjoyed him; I admired him; I trusted him. And he made me laugh for fifty-one years. Of course it wasn't fifty-one perfect years. Someone once asked John, "How long have you been married?" He answered, "Forty-five years - which comes to about forty-three years of wedded bliss." (You know, a bad weekend here; a bad month there. . .)

When he died nine years ago I fell into deep depression several times over the next five years. In between depression, and for the following four years I lived with heavy melancholy. A friend suggested a man she thought I should meet and I waved the idea aside - "After John?" The only reason I went on living was that there were people who loved me, who would have been crushed if I had ended my life, including my beloved son and his wonderful wife; three siblings who were my support team; and several dear friends. They all phoned and visited and took me out and helped me go on living. I made no effort to meet new people and turned down all party invitations. During the nine years I would not once have thought, "Life is good."

Melancholy

We all get melancholy soon enough
It's hard to walk through life when times are tough
You wonder where and what you'll do with life
Will I succeed, stand fast, support a wife
Will I even look beyond the ugliest of doubts
Let humor help you out of this depression
Laugh and let your mind hear this expression
The world is sad, funny, everywhere you look
Laugh within yourself, have some empathy
For many worse than you, have sympathy
You will find you are no worse off than most
Trading places? Don't give up that ghost.
    So don't complain, laugh your way through strife
    Cut melancholy swiftly from your life.

My days were spent alone. Each morning I completed a 16-across sudoku. The afternoons I read books, usually re-reading the classics or histories I always loved. I worked large jigsaw puzzles on the dining room table. Before bed I did crossword puzzles or acrostics or variety puzzles. A solitary, reclusive life. I avoided listening to music because the memories were too painful. I gave away all my old vinyl records and most of my CD's.

Only The Lonely

Whose heart conceals the loneliness of night?
Whose life will reveal what the heart may show?
My love is gone and will not come again.
Will there be more? None but the lonely know.

Think not of yourself; be happy with your friends
They all would help but afraid, so afraid to show
You must try but do not let the night descend
They may ask how you are, but only the lonely know.

Someday soon a light may open up your eyes
A face, a smile, a joy you have not known
Your life can change but you must make it so
Can you change yourself? None but the lonely know.

Come take that chance, new love may come your way
Your friends will smile as they watch your smile grow
Your world will change beyond the veil of the past
What went before the veil? Only the lonely know.

The kindness of family and friends kept me going. Among those friends were Ed and Joan Schwartz. Ed and my John had become friends playing pool on Saturday mornings at Lake Barrington Shores. Ed had been writing poetry but hadn't yet published any of his work. John loved Ed's writing, and a couple of times Ed brought new poems to our house to read to us. When John discovered he had inoperable pancreatic cancer, Ed was the second one we told here in Lake Barrington. He wrote a poem about friendship that he dedicated to John, and I asked Ed to read it aloud at John's memorial.

Ed began a pattern of phoning me every few months to make sure I was all right. He and Joan had me over for dinner, and another time I invited them for dinner. And at a later date when I had done a couple of new paintings that I was proud of, I invited them to come for the viewing. We began a pattern of lending books to each other, and discussing them over the phone. For instance, they had me read "The Shack" and wanted my take on it. And I lent the epic poem "John Brown's Body" by Steven Vincent Benet, and was very happy at how much Ed enjoyed it - because he is the only person I ever met who has read it - a book I consider the great American masterpiece - that no one has heard of.

I did not once think of Ed separately from Joan. They were my much valued book-loving friends. Well, I have to admit that something stirred in me when I read Ed's first book of poetry. But from long habit, that feeling was quickly suppressed.

Friends

We both lost our partners
As some of us must
We know what we're feeling
It overcomes us.

We have to move on
And not let our mien
Show our distress
To the popular scene.

It is then that a friend
From Lake Barrington Shores
A friend that understands
What we've been through,

Says, "Let those days go
And turn to your friends.
They will understand
They're a means to an end."

Even our children
Sometimes forget
Mom and Dad miss them
Send more than regrets.

Mother's day, Father's day
What do they glean
Alone by yourself
You'll know what I mean.

Now we're together
One more glass of wine
Happy Mother's day to you
We're both feeling fine.

In 2012 I wrote to Ed and Joan, sharing with them an email John had sent me describing what he saw on a rainy day on the lake. Ed turned John's note into a poem and put it into *Tapestry Two* along with an explanation of where it came from.

Recently I found, going through old emails, that Ed occasionally sent me a new poem. One in 2018 was *A Kiss in Winter.* I wrote back how much I liked it, and how well I remember my first kiss - and the first kiss John gave me.

May 20, 2019, was Ed's 83rd birthday. I sent him an email copying lines of one of his poems.

> You see beauty where some do not.
> You see colors that can light a flame.
> You see humor in your morning walk,
> And you see sadness passing through life's frame.

In June 2019 I held a garage sale. Ed came and bought a few things, including "the mystery box" – coins and tiny things John collected back in the 1940's when he was a kid. Also a group of photos of our sailboat on Lake Michigan. He came the second day also, bought something else, pulled up a chair and stayed for a visit.

That autumn I learned that Joan was going downhill. I didn't know about her fall on Christmas Day that put her in the hospital, and then into rehab, and then hospice. I knew from Ed's book of poems that her eightieth birthday was coming Feb. 14, 2020. I sent a birthday card, including wishes for a Happy Valentine's Day. Ed phoned to tell me that she could not respond; in fact that he couldn't even share the card with Joan. He said he knew the end was near. She would not or could not eat, and was slipping away.

He phoned me a few times in March and April to report on Joan's condition. Always downhill. I sent him Shakespeare's sonnet "Love is not love which alters when alteration finds..." His love for her was constant and unfailing.

The Last Romantics

There is no romance in an iPhone
Your partner can't see if you're kneeling
You can text "Where are you, whatcha doing?"
But can you text "I love you" with feeling?

It seems that romancing is dead
As you walk with your nose in the phone
And what have you learned about women
Or your boss, fellow workers, I groan.

Romance is not a touchable thing
Can't feel it if you removed a glove
It can light up your life forever
And romance can lead to love.

But what of true love, is it real?
Or just lust from the springtime of youth
After lust comes many new changes
The babies, the love and the truth.

Families are born through love and lust
New things then dominate the scene.
There's Howie and Debbie, good health and bad
The house and the car and the dream.

The children grow up and leave the house
Then there may be one more chance
If we are still there, if our hands do clasp
Will we still have the time for romance?

Our hair's gone gray, our youth just gone
Romance and love, are they really true?
If we're still together there is more time
I reach out my hand and touch you.

———

7

I still see the girl with the twinkling eyes
Though we are older and not quite so frantic
I'll bring you roses, poetry and music.
Let's do it again, the Last Romantics.

On April 8, 2020, Ed's beloved Joanie died. He had gone out on an errand and when he came back the "Visiting Angel" told him she was gone. It was a perfect afternoon for such news - extremely dark out with heavy rain. He phoned to tell me. Covid prevented a funeral and she was buried in Shalom Cemetery on a dreary, dark day. Two days later my sister Fran died suddenly; and because of my own great loss, I could not reach out to help Ed, but I well knew what he was going through. The pain. The tears. The loneliness of the empty rooms.

I wrote to my surviving sister Barb:

"I am very sad tonight. Joanie's and Fran's deaths bring back so many hard memories. My eyes have been wet all evening. But I have yet to hard-cry for over twelve years. I broke down three times in my life - but I did not cry when I learned John was dying, nor did I cry when and after he died. The only explanation I have is that it was so catastrophic in comparison with other sorrows that crying became trivial. Either that, or perhaps all emotion died with John. I still feel that my life ended when his life ended. I go thru the motions, I make plans, I do stuff. But ....

I won't share these thoughts with Ed when he calls again. He is a great optimist, and I think he can foresee a future life."

Ed called to tell me about the burial. He and his wife's sister and one friend were the only ones there, with the rabbi. Ed sang a verse of their favorite song (I can't imagine being able to do that), and read a poem Joan wrote to him and a poem he wrote to her. The rabbi did his thing, and that was that. Sad and lonely.

Sleep

When comes my time
I'm laid to rest
Before you leave
Give me one test

Press your lips
To my lonely brow
And if I move
Just ask me how

If I don't
Then say goodbye
When I am gone
Just let me lie

In an open field
With trees nearby
I never thought
That I would die

No prayers for me
My love is deep
Just lay me down
And let me sleep.

He called me to read two poems he wrote that week - both sad and bleak. *"Silence of Time"* and *"Mountain Top."* These two poems were printed in *"Tattered Tapestry."*

I finally called Ed - for the very first time - the third week in April. He said he would drop the two new poems off at my door. I told him no one had been here and I haven't been out

- how about risking a visit in this age of covid. He did and stayed three hours. Along with some tears, we had a lot of laughs and reminiscences, being the same age and remembering *"Student Prince"* and *"Kismet"* and Cole Porter and other good things. He said for the last two years he couldn't go out - couldn't go to a restaurant or the theater or anywhere except a few happenings at Lake Barrington Shores. And now that he is free, because of the virus there are no restaurants or theaters to go to. Irony.

Phone calls became more frequent. Near the end of April he came over to bring me a book. We decided to go to the Botanic Gardens when it opens. His hobbies have all been cancelled due to covid: he played pool (cancelled), bowled (cancelled), belonged to three book clubs (cancelled). The things that could help him right now have all been cancelled.

He brought me a CD to enjoy, and it is truly special - called *"George Gershwin Alone."* Hershey Felder, a very talented pianist, tells the story of Gershwin's life in the first person on disc 1, playing his music as if Felder/Gershwin were composing it. Disc 2 he plays *"Rhapsody in Blue,"* and then has the audience sing with him some of the most well known songs. The audience was spectacular. He picked out a few wonderful voices and asked them to sing the verses before the next songs. He picked out a couple of jazz voices, and asked them to sing *"Summertime"* together, improvising as they felt like it. One was alto and the other high soprano. Their duet sent chills up my spine.

Ed called early in May to ask if he could come over. He brought a book and I returned a book to him. I suggested he look thru my bookshelves and choose what he wanted. He chose the biography of Edna St. Vincent Millay and a collection of poetry my brother Tom gave me. Instead of a long afternoon, the time passed quickly and he left at 5.

I wrote to my sister: "Ed is not my future. I am good for him right now and I am enjoying his company. But it will be temporary."

May 11. I emailed Ed,

"I bought a pot of shade plants to put on my deck, but I will have to put them up on my balcony instead. Robins have chosen my deck for a nest. I noticed a few twigs on the outside lamp yesterday and wondered about it. Today it was a complete nest. And this evening I saw a robin sitting on it. I won't disturb them by putting the plants out. I plan to watch every few hours in the next few days until I see tiny birds with begging beaks. I know it is only a couple of weeks before they will be gone. Then I will put the plants out and enjoy my deck again. Until then, I feel I have been given a special gift. So, I just wanted to share with you ...

Robins never seem to grow old. The ones on my deck could be the same ones I saw when I was a child."

Ed wrote back, "Rebirth. The cycle goes on."

May 16. I wrote my sister,

"I haven't said much about Ed in the last week or two. But we talk on the phone almost every day and he comes by maybe every three days, exchanging books and sharing writings. We took a long walk today and found, as always, much to talk about. It will never come to anything more than friendship, but it is a good friendship. He stayed for dinner one evening. And today I asked if he has any plans for his birthday next week. No. Would he like to have dinner here? He said there is nothing he would like better.

A Glass Of Wine

We won't speak about the years
Or the birthdays that have passed
Let's just think of where we are
No choice, alone again at last.

This spring's been good for nature
Everything is blooming through
Just want to spend the day walking, talking
Listening, seeing, drinking nature's view.

The grass, the trees, the flowers
A performance without end
Except the time for hibernation
When the snows will come again.

For now this lovely spring
Is slipping into summer time
Let's just stay and watch the show
Nature's glow,
    and drink a glass of wine.

A few people here might be shocked. It is just over a month since Joan died. But this friendship is the same as two women or two men. Support at a time of sorrow. Two people who truly understand sorrow.

He mentioned a poem that he wrote when Joan was dying - saying that the memories will fade. I assured him they will not, and that he won't want them to. He was listening to some Gershwin songs today, in tears, and again I assured him that will not end, and he won't want it to."

May 18. We took a walk around the top of the lake, North Bay, and into the forest preserve. So much to talk about.

A Walk

An early Sunday morning, warm for May
I took a stroll around the lake today
Willows waving wildly to the passerby
They paint a new Matisse against the sky
Nets of golden leaves, spread about the trees
The sun was shining brightly in my eyes
And suddenly a song I've never heard
Came playfully from a passing yellow bird
Whose mate did pick the tune from his song
As I walked my feet touched not the way
I found my life at peace in nature's sway
When a little boy, with fishing pole in hand
    Completed now the picture in my mind.
    Reminds me of a youth in another time.

May 20, Ed's birthday. The robin allowed us to have a glass of wine on the deck before dinner. I made a crockpot beef recipe. Ed brought the dessert or I would have bought a birthday cake. Home-made chocolate mousse with a white vanilla cream sauce on top. Wonderful.

We have assigned that birthday evening to the beginning of our new relationship. He jokes that he was "the man who came to dinner..."

May 21. I wrote, "Today is a perfect spring day. From my balcony door comes the gorgeous scent of fresh cut grass and mock orange blossoms. Robins and a new warbler pair are serenading me. I am actually going to a party tomorrow on the large driveway of some old friends. BYOB and BYOC (chair)."

It was the last party I went to alone.

May 26. Memorial Day. I spent the day with Ed. Neither of us had anything to do or anywhere to go. We talked for four hours sitting on the deck and in the living room. So comfortable, including the silences. I feel so fortunate to have this friendship.

May 31, Ed phoned at 4 saying it is a beautiful afternoon, let's take a walk. Well, it was close to 5 when we got back. Wine time. He said he was hoping I would ask him in for wine. Then it was close to supper time and yes, he was hoping I would ask to stay for dinner. He finally left about 8:30. He is such easy company.

Swiftly

A tiny swift
Finds its wings
Slips into the fearful sky
Not sure he touches down
Something says he has to fly
But why?

He sees another swift
And imitates its flight
An insect passes by
He turns his head swiftly
And now he knows why
His mother passes by
She sees he understood
And it was good.

He spies a little boy
And steers ahead
A pole and lure trying
To imitate his dad
Herky, jerky cast
But he was glum
The lure, bigger
Than his thumb.

An old man needlessly asked
"Do you want to catch one?"
A nod and, "Yes, Sir," he said
His eyes lit like the sun.

He swiftly got a hook and worm
A bobber for the boy
He cast it out, not far
And waited for the joy.

To sit and wait
Is not the fate of
Little boys of brown
But soon the bobber moved
And suddenly went down.

Then there was a bluegill
His very, very first fish
He ran down to his father
"Dad! Dad, I got my wish!"

Dad is proud,
Sister wants to play
The old man trundles off
He has had a very good day.

Next week he will drop off a stack of new poems I will proofread before publication. First was *"Tapestry"*; then *"Tapestry Two."* This will be *"Tattered Tapestry,"* mostly written since Joan died. I have read and heard several. I believe he is writing his best work this year

On June 3rd I wrote my sister: "June 8 will be the first time in 60 years that I will celebrate a birthday without family. Last year [my sister] Fran came for the weekend. The only person I see frequently is Ed; all other friends are scared of covid. So he asked what I would like to do on my birthday, and I said, "I'd like to go to Morton Arboretum. It is opening just for members from June 1-15."

The weather looked promising, so I joined, becoming a member just so I can go on June 8. I couldn't get the computer to take my request for 1 pm, so I phoned. I have learned many things from my sister Fran, and one of the most valuable is how to play pitiful. Here's what happened.

On the phone the pleasant woman said she would email my confirmation for one person. I said make it for two because I am bringing a friend. She explained at this time, members only. I played pitiful ... I explained it would be my 85th birthday and I want to spend it at the Arboretum, but I can't come alone because I can't drive. I have to come there with my driver. She said "No problem - at the gate just tell them he's your caregiver."

I phoned Ed and told him. This was truly funny because he was his wife's caregiver for ten years, and she required constant care during this last year of her life. And now next Monday he'll be a designated "caregiver" all over again.

June 8. The day at the Arboretum was beautiful. We took a few photos, ate sandwiches in a picnic pavilion, and drove the slow miles through the trees. Ed wrote a poem about the day.

The Morton Arboretum

We walked the trails at Morton
The sun beaming through the trees
Left dots of dappled sunlight
Always changing, and a cooling breeze.

There's no smell like a forest
Made from leaves and bark and earth
All melded into perfumed odors
Of which only nature can give birth.

I'm reminded of those early days
When few people were around
The trees abound, they grow, they die
They fall and fertilize the ground.

It is then the seedling sees his chance
And begins his humble climb
It will take him many years
But the trees have all the time.

I love the beauty of the trees
All their forest friends and stars
The man-shaped giant on his back
A giant squirrel throwing rocks at cars.*

What creatures are these
Made of wood and straw?
Don't belong in these woods
Send them back to Mackinaw.

---

* At the Morton Arboretum, someone had created giant trolls out of sticks and other natural materials. They were a delight to children and photographers.

I ask the world to let them be
A place like this should forever stand
If we ever lose the trees
Then all of us will lose this land.

June 11. ZaZa's opened tonight with a big outdoor tent. I went with Ed (dutch) and the owner came out and said we were the first ones to be seated in the tent so our drinks were on the house. It was so good to be back. Lobster ravioli for the first time in months! Ed wants to go to the Elgin Symphony this fall and winter. I have only been there once before.

June 13. Just got back from Kohl's after a walk by the lake with Ed. I see him almost every day now. And he calls average of twice a day. The relationship is as comfortable as an old shoe. We've had dinner together at least twice a week. I don't know where it's going, but the trip is very pleasant.

Ed has been writing nonstop. He told me the other day he actually feels happy because for the first time in ten years he is free - and can do anything he wants. No one reading his poetry could ever doubt he adored Joan. But he was an exhausted caregiver for the last ten years.

And he is still a caregiver. He has a 93-year-old neighbor who recently took a fall. He brings her coffee each morning and takes her trash cans out. Her kids just sent him a very warm thank you note.

If this very fine friendship lasts, I will be very fortunate.

June 14. I wrote to my sister:

" I am falling in love with Ed. It is unexpected. Unwanted. Unreasonable. Disturbing. And incredibly sweet. I invited him for dinner and after dinner we sat and listened to Donald Shirley's gorgeous piano music. He asked, with a shaky voice, 'Are we too old to hold hands?' I took his hand in both of mine, gratefully, joyfully. And there we sat for an hour, quietly loving the music. I believe the feelings are mutual."

When the music ended he asked if he should stay or go. I said time to go.

We all know the wisdom of "make no changes in your life for a year." But people our age also remember *"September Song."*

Other people may be very uncomfortable and very concerned about this. It is just two months since Joan died. But love is happening. I feel as lost and scared as I did when I was falling in love with John sixty years ago.

There would be no point in anyone trying to give me advice. It is what it is. But I was so glad I had my surviving sister to talk to.

June 15. We watched the second half of the opera *"Porgy and Bess"* tonight. And I told him that I know it is too soon for him, but I needed to tell him - that I love him. I used the words from *"September Song"* - "I haven't got time for the waiting game." I would say his reaction was happy. We talked and laughed, even joking about which religion would we raise the kids. He said as he was leaving that he believes we have a wonderful life ahead. And at the door, "Goodnight, my love."

I can't believe this - I truly never expected to be happy again. He reminded me that for the eight years after John died he phoned me a few times a year, simply because he liked me as a friend. Yes, I told him I really appreciated those calls.

I wrote: "I'm rambling. I didn't fall asleep until 4 am last night. But now that I have said the words to him, and heard his response, I think I will sleep well tonight."

Who would have thought?

June 16. An email from Ed was waiting for me in the morning. It was the first sonnet ever written to me, and the most delightful I have ever read.

Fate

Who is that man with the smile on his face?
Said my mirror to the glass shower door
Looks a little like the guy who lives here
I've never seen that happy smile before
Could it be there's been a change in his life
What could transform a man when he's eighty-four?
Most men that age would find a senior home
Sit back, relax and simply write a poem.
I had a date with fate, only been sixty years
I felt for a while some old teenage fears
But I touched her hand and she touched me back
    As scared as I was I felt young and strong.
    She turned and she laughed, "What took you so long?"

That day we took a walk at Cuba Marsh. I cooked dinner for us, and we listened to Rachmaninoff after dinner.

During the hard days of deep depression, a very fine psychiatrist helped me. He said, "There is a light at the end of the tunnel, but there is a bend in your tunnel and you can't see the light." I never believed I would see light again. I think the last time I felt this happy was John's and my 20th anniversary at Door County, forty years ago.

Late that night Ed sent me another poem by email, *"Love, Covid and Old Age."*

Love, Covid And Old Age

This is the troubled day
With lovers on the scene
Then comes the troubled night
With social distancing.

How can we all exist
When touching turns to shame
We cannot love tonight
Tomorrow is the same.

There is a way 'round covid scene
The old are getting bolder
Just put your arms around my neck
And mine around your shoulder.

You may have time, the old man said
Social distance is not convincing.
The time is now, at eighty-five,
I have no time for listening.

The next morning he sent another, *"Love in Your Eighties."*

Love In Your Eighties

Old age is kinder to some
I feel my life is changing
I've found another who matches my life
Now I don't feel like I'm aging.

Happened like lightning, did not see it coming
Summer storm blowing, it's windy and raining
Cleansing the earth, clearing my mind
Look at me, eighty-four, I'm not complaining.

I cannot say this too often
The feelings I've found are so new
Past is still there, behind a veil
I just know, my dear, I'll always love you.

I wrote him: "After another sleepless night I was suddenly wondering if I have taken advantage in your time of bereavement. You are, after all, the most eligible bachelor at LBS. I wonder if you have even mentioned us to your counselor because we both know what a counselor would advise. Slow down. A half year. A year. For me I love being caught in this tsunami. Thrilled and joyous and filled with love for you. But if you need some breathing space, you must take it."

June 17. Ed's red SUV is parked in my driveway every evening. Now that my next-door neighbor has seen us on the deck, she knows whose car it is. She has known Ed longer than I, going back to when her husband and Ed were both on the master board.

We have talked the serious talk now - sex, marriage, finances, health, children - (as in which religion shall we raise the children?)

(Just kidding.) We decided that for economic reasons, and inheritance to our offspring, marriage was not a good idea. I wrote to my son, "Our interests are so similar sometimes we laugh at the consistency of it. Big band music; 50's jazz; classical music; classical novels; all the same movies; the love of birds, gardens, forests. And travel."

Late that night he sent me another new poem, *"Second Time Around"*.

The Second Time Around

The wellspring of love, for all to partake
But many do not, for they're not aware
That love is more than just a brief affair
Not kiss or hug with coffee, morning break
Not the lust of boys and girls on their first date.
Too many rush to marriage and don't know
That character and kindness are first rate.
If you hope for long marriage with your mate
Prepare yourself, you have chosen sorrow
Make plans, my friends, night is dark tomorrow
Sometimes late in life you'll find a second love
Old age is tricky but sometimes gives a shove
    Some very close friends I know have lately found
    Love can be lovelier the second time around.

June 18. Ed sent me another sonnet, *"You Have Chosen,"* using my grandfather's counsel to me sixty years ago, "Ah, Mary, so you have chosen to know sorrow."

You Have Chosen

Time for marriage, happiest day of your life
Life and love evermore, your children, your wife
Can't get better, culmination it seems
Of the years in school, your work and your dreams.
In sickness and health, remember that line
Before you find wealth there will come a time
The children are sick, the job is too tough
Not serious, we hope, times do get rough
Your lives are not story books, sorrow is there
Sometimes there's death, and sometimes despair
These are the things that could happen to you
We hope that they don't, but nothing is true
    And child, when you say "I do" tomorrow
    Remember, you have chosen to know sorrow.

The red SUV was still in the driveway the morning of June 19. And the 20th. And now for good. My neighbor told us we are the talk of Indian Point Road.

The Painter, The Poet And The Piano

Lost my endless love, tried to paint his face
My fingers would not work, color was not there
Thought my life was over, faded into air
Piano would not listen, notes came out all wrong
Sat down in despair, waiting for his song
Read some poems from a book I purchased late
That brought chills and warmth to my sorry state
His voice touched my mind, brought color to my heart
It was not my lover's song but possibly a start
As fate would seal, his love was gone this time
I changed my life and invited him to dine
He came at will, we drank a glass of wine
    When he touched my hand, music came out fine
    My piano found its tune; the poet now is mine.

Ed and I were both faithful to our vows made sixty-some years ago. We will be faithful to the vows we have newly made to each other. We will cherish each other until "death do us part."

One year later, a P.S.

I have been so fortunate in love - twice in one lifetime. I love Ed; I like him; I enjoy him; I admire him; I trust him. And he has made me laugh for the whole year.

CHAPTER 2

For those of you who have read *"Tattered Tapestry,"* the third book of the Tapestry trilogy, you have read of the pain and sorrow that Ed experienced with the loss of his beloved Joanie. The following poems are a continuation of the expression of that loss, and the surprise of finding new love.

Tapestry Renewed

The tapestry we wove is old and tattered
We built the life we lived, it was our dream
At the time it seemed t'was all that mattered
Not knowing one must fall beside the stream
The river of life takes and gives as pleases
No help from man, or changing of seasons
River leaves flood, life and death in its wake
Will those that live step up or will they quake?
For you who live, the world is for your taking
Open your eyes, there's someone there to love
You choose to live or go on pretending
Or live your life, what's left, without ending.
    Find purpose and love and go on giving
    Just turn, touch a hand and go on living.

July 19, 2020

In This Silence

In this silence of my life
Nothing else to do but write
I cannot see tomorrow nor today
I can but see inside of me
And all the days of yesterday
I hear the words, they strike a chord
And as my inner self pushes
Should I let it be and grow
From earth like trees and bushes
No wife to help me write divine
Nothing interferes with poetry
Except perhaps a thirst for wine.
Write on, poet, it's all on lend
Time will bend, then I will end.

May 10, 2020

It's Been Fun

Every beat of your heart
Every tick of the clock
It's just slipping away
That's always a shock.

Every moment in time
Every day of the year
As time marches on
The answer is clear.

Your time will be up
It's a very short race
I just can't keep up
I'll fall on my face.

I cannot believe
The years that have flown
My friends and my enemies
Nothing but bone.

The time has come
Train leaves at five
Nobody gets out
Of this life alive.

Goodbye to you all
My friends and my love
I leave you forever
I'll watch from above.

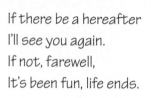

If there be a hereafter
I'll see you again.
If not, farewell,
It's been fun, life ends.

September 19, 2020

I Miss Her So

In the days that I have left
I walk so slow, I walk alone
Because my heart has turned to stone
And I would rather walk alone.
    Because I miss her so.

I don't want to pray
Play golf or bowl
There is just no feeling
In my heart, in my soul.
    I miss her so.

One child gone, the other away
Find little to do at start of day
Grandchildren okay, but far away
What shall I do today?
    I miss her so.

First stop moaning about what was
Start thinking about what is
Depression won't help any one here
Just say you miss her, go on with your biz.
    And still miss her so.

The business of living each day as it comes
You might pay some bills, lean on your friends
Meet someone new, lonely people out there
You'll find out that life has more than its end.
    And you can still miss her so.

May 28, 2020

As We Disappear

Life may disintegrate, water on stone
A lifetime will come and then will be gone
Regardless of size, regardless of health
Life has one duty, perpetuate itself
But there has to be more, look at our lives
From youngsters to teens, we marry our mates
And as we grow older we bury our greats
We've done our duty, had children and then
Some get creative the older they get
Some just lie down awaiting their death
Listen to us while you still have us here
Speak to your elders, they have stories to share
    We've lived out our lifetimes, nothing to fear
    Speak now or miss us. . . as we disappear.

September 5, 2020

Walk With Me

Walk with me while I age
Talk to me as I grow old
Look and see that I am here
Don't leave me in the cold.

Write to me, if you can
Listen to my tales, my dear
As long as I am able to speak
Tell me I have nothing to fear.

Why are we here, family and years
Why am I here, where did they go
Walk with me, dear, while I age
My hair is the color of snow.

I fell again yesterday, just missed a step
How did I fall, nothing is broke
Doctor said, "Nothing is wrong"
At least I know it wasn't a stroke.

But let us not worry, I asked you here
To walk and to talk about family and friends.
Is Bob still around and Gena and Jen?
I know, but when you leave, I'll forget it again.

But if you just talk with me
Please hold my hand and see
And if you just walk with me
Perhaps a cup of tea.

September 21, 2020

Walk With Me While I Age

Walk with me while I age
Old folks today are not the rage
Young folks don't talk to old folks
But the old folks are leaving the stage.

So much we can give to the youngsters
But they don't believe that we know much
If only they knew what we know
Maybe something in us they can touch.

The young say, "We're smarter than you are,
We're smarter than everyone old,"
Then one day the electricity went off
The young were left out in the cold.

So walk with me as I age
Walk with me as I drink my cup
And then, my fine young friends,
I'll talk to you ... when you grow up.

September 21, 2020

Dust To Dust

I feel the dust of centuries
Gather round me as I walk
Dust includes pieces of time
What would it say if it could talk.

Pieces of me drift away in the dusk
They float away on currents of air
They disappear as they touch the ground
Or add to the dust on the chair.

Lives we have touched with sandaled foot
This once was a working man
Or woman, or child, or the world
All of these turn into sand.

We live our lives not thinking
Of those who have gone before
In peaceful death or sickness
Or maybe accident or war.

Are we dust for future generations
Will they do better and use some restraint
Will they build upon the things we've done
Will they walk on our remains?

Ashes to ashes, dust to dust
It all goes on and through.
Your dust, my dust, drifts on down
The answer? Time's dust is you.

July 16, 2019

Bend In The Road

Long and dusty road, followed to the end
Unpaved, of course, until you see the bend.
From childhood, road is smooth until you see
Side roads you can take, so starts the mystery.
You will not know which road is best, but choice
Is life's gift to you; there will not be a voice
That says, "This side road is the best for you."
All that easy learning now comes into view
You wonder if all those dreams will come true.
To those of us who made that trip, so old
Found that few, if any, roads were paved with gold.
And if you've lost your love along the way
    You may think there is nothing left to say.
    That final bend may lead to to a brand new day.

November 24, 2020

36

Covid And Love

By myself again after all those years
I had no place to go to hide my tears
Think I'll fish Key West for about a year
Haven't left my house in a very long time
I want to disappear from my own mind
But Covid held me back, I dare not go
The woman, also, could not travel, so
She stayed at home not knowing what to do
My birthday loomed, she called me on that day.
If you have no plans, I know your month is May.
There really was no other choice to say
The time, the date, the place was not hard sell.
 We found we fit together and we fell
 And so in fact did Covid treat us well.

November 10, 2020

What I Thought Was Lost

What I thought was lost has been returned again
The dawn of day with arms entwined and then
The easy touch of lips that says you're still alive
The silly wonder of coffee or dessert
The quick laugh when remembering last night's tide
Which carried us to space and what a ride
And back on earth the early morning time
When you reach back and feel how life can rhyme
Those days and times were gone forever in your mind
When suddenly a lifeline intertwined
Her name was Mary and she had not a clue
That you and she would be one stead of two
  That you and she would light your way to history
  At eighty-five, one of nature's mysteries.

        October 23, 2020

Hold Her Hand

The breeze embraced, as I would you
I felt your love by counting stars
I touched your hand and kissed your lips
And then I knew the joy was ours.

The shoots of spring as they turned green
Our love has grown from that June day
There never was a greater love
Than what I felt, I have to say.

If ever you do get the chance
If ever you want to feel grand
Turn to her, the girl you love,
"Am I too old to hold your hand?"

November 28, 2020

Loveland

Welcome to the land of mirth, joy and love
Where is this land you ask of me above?
I cannot tell you where or if you'll come
The journey must be made by two in love
You won't be alone, all the world will watch
Some may founder before they start, that's so
But those who come on their own will know
An ecstasy great as any found in life
Be it man or woman, friend, husband, wife
You hold her in your arms, an aura of light
Then washes over like a passing storm
You've found the land of nowhere, sheer delight
    Suppose you think it's only for the young, Matey,
    Well shiver me timbers, for I am over eighty.

November, 2020

Love

Love is a journey beyond belief
It lifts up your heart, it tickles your toes
Breath of fresh air, a thrill down your spine
Tickles a side, it senses your nose,

Your senses go infinite, gravity's gone
Your body twists inward, your head is afloat
Your fingers tingle, you shiver and shake
Legs make you shaky, they're rocking the boat.

You feel you are falling, stout arms hold you up
Drawn into a vortex his arms are your might.
A quick trip to Saturn, an amazing day
You've fallen in love and everything's right.

A sense of completeness engulfs your whole being
Your face wants to smile and then comes the laugh
You don't want to leave, he won't let you go
Life is complete; you've found the other half.

July 12, 2020

Looks Are Not Everything

There may be wrinkles upon your face
Don't let them extend to your heart
What's inside your head is more important
Than the looks you were born with impart.
Love doesn't care what you look like today
Your intelligence does not give a whit
The eyes that you prize dream not of deceit
The nose that you know is just there to breathe
Each one has a beauty that needs to be found
It's there, somewhere, listen to the sound
Of someone, somewhere, discovering their way
Their wrinkles are gone, delightful to say.
    Feel the thrill, release your bonds from the ground
    Looks are not everything, your hands are not bound.

November 8, 2020

Fountain Of Youth

Ponce de Leon searched the world wide
He searched for the Fountain of Youth
He wanted to be made young again
But he searched in vain for the truth.

If he really wanted to be young again
He would bring his lady a dove
And tell her then, the Fountain of Youth
Is really the Fountain of Love.

November 24, 2020

Could This Be Verse

I leave to all what they will think of me
How I led my life, what I want to be
Leave them all the joy God has granted me
My love I give to all, mostly to my wife
Who brought to me the joy of living life
With all things new that let me live my wishes
Uninterrupted music from my vinyls,
Harmony of home, as I wash the dishes,
Concert halls and travel, if we wish it
And so much more I didn't know existed.
I cannot sing or play a melody,
Yet I can write, but how to end this poem?
    I must step back a touch to just rehearse
    This poem I give to you - Could this be verse?

November 11, 2020

Love Stories

The greatest love stories
Are told and retold
Romeo and Juliet
Just leave me cold.

Cleopatra had her problems
With her Tony, don't ask
And with Caesar before
Such trouble, perhaps an asp.

Princess Merkle told Harry
What she was about
Queen Liz, always smart
Had plenty of doubt.

Star crossed they were
Ed gave up his throne
He loved his Wally
And they both went home.

So don't have your doubts
If you find your princess
Just treat her with kindness
And love you won't miss.

When love stories are told
Of kings, queens and stars
You'll look back and say
The best love story is ours.

July 10, 2020

The Woman Who Waited For Me

As darkness closes down the day
A view in front of me prevails
A lake of thriving greens and blues
A cardinal and a boat with sails.

The view is lovely, nature's delight
But there's more to life than seeing
To reach out and touch a hand
Keep a man and woman believing.

Life's path has encountered many forks
Each turn you make brings your fate
You cannot know which way is right
But you will find it's never too late.

When day is done, your mate is gone
Your children are doing their thing
If fate slips open the door once more
Don't wait, fate's smile may bring

A second love, so few get a chance
To open a new life, a new season
Take her into your arms, give her a kiss
For second loves, no rhyme or reason.

June 22, 2020

All The Time In The World

Time means nothing to the young
They run and jump and play
Age is just a random number
The sum of all their days.

Age is not significant
Too young to feel the fool
Time begins to mean much more
As now they enter school.

The divisions then are obvious
They begin to feel time
From grammar through to high
They start that fearful climb.

College soon will beckon
Education has just begun
Before they know what happened
They reach that fateful twenty-one.

Now they begin to worry
They see life passing by
Time now means something
They buckle down and try.

But time remains mysterious
You now may meet the one
Who lulls you with a blanket of love
At thirty-one, a daughter and son.

My God, where did the time go
My life is a flag unfurled
I never thought I'd say this but
I had all the time in the world.

My daughter's getting married
The thought gives me a chill
I'm not ready to be a grandpa
Not sure I ever will.

The road leads on, the children gone
The house too big, don't need the space
I'm here alone, why don't they call?
Find something to do or lose the race.

When we were young there was no time
Growing up we discovered its speed
In later years it rocketed by
In older years we follow its lead.

Time at this stage has little meaning
Nor do we live for the social whirl.
We do our best near the century mark
For we have all the time in the world.

October 31, 2020

Pygmalion

He carved a likeness of woman so well
The King was enamored, in love he fell
But that would not do him, he could not dwell
With an ivory image, in vain he did blame
And then in a dream Aphrodite came
Brought ivory to life, she became his wife.
King's name was Pygmalion, the story begins
A beautiful girl who changes her life
From drab to beauty, at another man's whim
From the depth of cockney, she rises above
Changes her accent and then falls in love
With the man who taught her to speak and to move
    A tale with some caution, don't tempt the fate
    If you fall for your creation, she could be your mate.

(See the painting by Jean-Leon Gerome)

December 7, 2020

It Was A Very Good Song

When I was twenty-three
It was a very good year
I found a girl I loved for life
Who I took for my wife
There never was strife.
It was a very good year.

When I was fifty-three
It was a very good year
It was a very good year to celebrate
Thirty years in a wedded state
As I loved my mate.
It was a very good year.

When I was eighty-three
It was a fairly good year
It was a fairly good year to celebrate
Sixty years of bliss
That ended in a kiss
As I said goodbye, my dear,
We've had some very good years.

When I was eighty-five
It was a very good year
A lovely lady of means
Who liked the same things
Music, books and strings
I was satisfied.

And at eighty-five
It was a damn good year.

When Frank sang this song
It was a very good year
But something went wrong
Cause he ended the song
My age bracket was gone!
Perhaps I've lived too long.

It's still a very good song.

November 4, 2020

CHAPTER 3

Bert and I

The year was 1949. Bert Lucarelli and I were in the same class together at Morse Grammar School in Chicago. We were friendly but not true friends at the time. Then one week he didn't show up for classes. I learned later that he had been hit by a car and had broken both legs.

The teacher asked if anyone lived near Bert and could bring him his books and lessons so he could graduate next year with his class. I volunteered; Bert and I became great friends and he did graduate with our class in 1950. We then went to Austin High in Chicago together - that is, Bert and I, my sister Janice, and my 1938 Ford with mechanical brakes.

Having lost out on baseball, Bert took up playing oboe in the school orchestra. Our paths diverged, he into music and I into business. We never saw each other again. I heard, later on, that he was becoming well known in the New York scene playing oboe, but we had lost touch.

Skip ahead seventy years to 2020. I walked into a music store and there was this strange solo oboe album called, *"The Sensual Sound of the Soulful Oboe"* featuring Bert Lucarelli. I couldn't believe it. I bought it, took it home, and it was a beautiful recording. The last song on the record was *"Estrellita,"* my mom's favorite song. She had played it over and over back in the 1940's.

So I checked the internet and sure enough, Bert had become famous as an oboe recitalist, teacher, and was known world wide. Needless to say, I contacted him and we are having a great time talking about the past and dear old Morse Grammar School.

I have written three poems for and about Bert. The first, *"Life Is Not a Waltz,"* came from his book, *"You Can't Always Play Waltzes."* The second is about refreshing our friendship from seventy long years ago, *"Old Friends."* The third poem, *"Estrellita"* reminds me of my mom.

Life Is Not A Waltz

A man must work to keep his family fed
A musician must practice throughout the year
A dancer must constantly learn new steps
We can't always play waltzes, my dear.

A lover may wonder if his lady is true
A lady may wonder if her lover fears
A child needs a mother when things go wrong
We can't always play waltzes, my dear.

An official may whistle his way to work
And tonight find his daughter in tears
You may wish your vacation could start right now
We can't always play waltzes, my dear.

Don't wish, work hard and practice, my dear
And someday you may play waltzes all year.

October 23, 2020

Old Friend

He showed me an oboe his dad used to play
Said he hoped that he could play it someday
In high school he studied, practiced a lot
I was not into music, we drifted apart.
Seventy years later I entered a store
The Sensual Oboe on a CD I adored.
So Bert had made it, I learned that in time
A Solo Oboe and Bert, it all rhymed
Opened the internet, typed in his name
Lo, a full page for a friendship that waned.
He soon called me back, together again
We parted in Fifty-Two, not happy or sad
    Morse School never knew what students it had
    Poet, musician, two kids from Chicago.
    They made it. Not bad!

November 14, 2020

Estrellita (Little Star)

I could not know my mother pictured here
Her sad beauty overwhelms me even now
Many years to come before I thought of her
Why now sadness, do I wish to borrow?
I remember her soft caress as she
Hummed her first-born tenderly to bed
Humming softly as in *"Estrellita"*
Sleep well, little star, grow beyond the tread
Of marching feet, of broken bones and guns
May you be one of those that does return
Your mother's prayer, your father's wish
Then live your life with love and great concern.
    I hum this lovely song of Estrellita
    This wish, from your mother named Anyta.

January 18, 2021

CHAPTER 4

NATURE POEMS

*W*e live in a townhouse in Lake Barrington Shores, perhaps the loveliest of Chicago's gated condo communities - which few people have ever heard of. Living at LBS is like living in a gorgeous resort. We have our own private forest preserve; our own private sand beach and a marina that houses a pontoon boat for parties, along with kayaks, canoes, fishing boats, Sunfish sailboats and other small water craft available to all residents. We have an indoor and outdoor pool, fitness center, ballroom, party room and library. There is an 18-hole golf course here for members. The grounds and the lake are beautifully cared for, as is the forest preserve. The multitude of trees offer color in all seasons. If you are unfamiliar with Lake Barrington Shores, come out on any Sunday afternoon and pick up a list of open houses from the front gate. And welcome to a poet's paradise!

Ed and I look out in one direction on enormous maples and spruces, and in the other direction on the North Bay of Lake Barrington. We can watch the wildlife from a bedroom balcony, a dining room deck, and a lower level patio. We have a virtual aviary with four feeders attracting three kinds of woodpeckers, nuthatches, chickadees, cardinals, and of course the ubiquitous sparrows. Geese and ducks entertain us with their idiosyncrasies. We enjoy migrating loons, grebes, cormorants and sandhill cranes.

Each season has its own beauty and for the most part, the winter snows stay white and beautiful. After a freeze, snow on the lake will be crossed by deer and other wildlife.

The beauty and wonder of LBS has inspired Ed's poetry, day after lovely day.

Portrait From My Window

My window is an ever changing portrait
As the seasons come and go, early, late
No duplication in this show, always changes
Never changes, never boring but adoring
Describe the indescribable, don't try
To photograph the flight of a tiny fly
The sun ascends behind the forest trees
Its rays float out and touch the tips of leaves
Then spread and shatter in the waves of seas
The sky above, silver blue and soft light clouds
Or sometimes dark and heavy like a shroud
But every passing minute is so proud
    A play that only Mother Nature could arrange
    Only birds pay no attention to its change.

October 14, 2020

Sun

The sun will bring its warmth to this cold land
But somehow too much warmth may rue the day
A sun so strong that sunburn rapes the skin
And you may wish you never heard of sand
But when you see the sun in spring, how gentle
A touch on fallen seed or wakes the bear
That has to feed on bounty sun will share
Sap rising, tree, bush, leaf and berry bloom
Has heated up the earth for growth or death
Sahara sand so hot it takes away your breath
At sands of Iwo, where our soldiers bled
And left behind the lives each soldier led.
    The sun is good, the sun is bad, it is said
    Without sun, no you, no earth, no man could tread.

November 30, 2020

Great Blue Heron

An early morning watch from my own deck
I saw a shadow gliding toward North Bay
The mist exploded, body, wings and neck
A Great Blue Heron came to fish this day
She settled lightly, a spider on a fly
Drew in her wings that fit her sides so well
That she had any wings at all was hard to tell
I poured a touch of wine upon the earth
For seeing things too beautiful to see
Another drop of wine upon my tongue
This special sight that God has given me
Her neck extends beyond what man can see
    She stalks her prey in perfect harmony
    The angels watch her wings in jealousy.

July, 2020

A Thousand Woodpeckers

The quiet of a lovely country morning
Shattered by pictures falling off the walls
My gabled roof, so thin, had been a warning
A thousand woodpeckers, pecking on my roof
Seeking buried food or trying to attack
Or cloggers, twenty, dancing out a tract
And Cagney teaching someone how to hoof
I cannot leave the house this ugly day
My door is blocked by wooden slabs about
Material is falling from my rotten roof
They're digging in, my love, I can't get out
Call nine-one-one and give the boys a shout!
    But sounds begin to fade, the day does whine
    The roofers gone, new roof is looking fine.

May 22, 2020

Reign = Rain

The reign of the leaves is over
Equinox of fall has ended
Seasons have changed as usual
As the rain of leaves descended.

Fall slowly falls away
As winter's grip ascended
Winter is King Cold here
Until his reign has ended.

Old man winter, if left alone
Will fuss and fume and blizzard
Keeping winter a long time here.
The old man seems a wizard.

Queen Spring cannot fight winter
For many a day she sits
Her world is frozen and cold
But young spring uses her wits.

Old man winter, when he tires
He steps out and sleeps on the ice
And all of his falling temperatures
Remind him that ice is so nice.

Spring places a slice of sun
Under his bed of ice water
He relaxes and starts to fall asleep
"Mmmm - that feels better than it ought-er."

The king falls asleep and
Spring tiptoes through
The king whispers, in his sleep
"Next year I will get you."

Then the grass turns green
As the snow turns to rain
It's time for the leaves
To begin their new reign.

October 21, 2020

Always The Cycle

Sky is clear again
Earth sighs deeply
Smothered by sandstorms
She has slept weeping
Waiting for the pandemic
To destroy
This disease of humanity
Killing her by ploy

Airplanes are grounded
Birds find no impediments
To flight. Away from crowds
The earth breathes sediments
Creatures give birth
New generations pass
Fish thrive, but few
Achieve the art of
Touching grass.
Humans may shout
But stay in their burrows until
Authority allows them out.
What fools these mortals be.

A tiny virus
Lays them down
And now they can't
Get up; but should they?
No way to recant.

Puny virus, kill a million
Drop of water in the ocean

We will rise
Repeat our mistakes
No learning curve in sight
Humanity is the fake.
Those in charge are worse.
Learn from history
Or you are cursed.

A new planet, you say
The next and the next
The universe enumerates
Super Virus is on the way
Will it illuminate
Or is that indeterminate?

The earth sleeps
Will we have the humanity
To wake and stop
This scourge of insanity?
Take all the money
Spread it out to
All the world
Milk and honey
No one is poor or sad
People rejoice
They've all gone mad

The earth has no voice
Against a virus,
Or something worse
May come and curse
Humanity in its vanity.
And the cycle begins again.

May 8, 2020

Autumn

Late October dawned with a cold light frost
The flowers bent their heads at summer's loss
Fled to fall's surprise, sun peeked through a cloud
And found the maples burning red and gold
So rich the colors that my eyes behold
I turned away to see a flick of red
From a swiftly feeding, fleeing passing head.
Nuthatches, black caps try to eat the fall
Can they beat sparrows who really want it all
Flock of geese still eating grass from our lawn
Don't they know it's easier when the mower's gone
The passing scene is marvelous today
    With birds and grebes and hawks all flying by
    But soon old winter's snow will rule the sky.

October 23, 2020

Music Or Laughter

Music of the ages as heard from a bird
The beautiful sounds that float in the air
They all tell a story, not one with words
The hoot of an owl, the screech of a hawk,
The caw of a crow, or a chicken squawk.
The breeze in the trees, the ripples in a stream
The clouds in the sky searching for a dream
All tell us of something we all should know
Sometimes of storm, sometimes of snow,
A tinkle of laughter that comes with the fear
God may be laughing as we struggle through
The sounds and the music slide by our ears.
    We find love in laughter. What are the odds
    That laughter is, the music of the gods.

August 4, 2020

Willow

This stately willow was once a seed
A seed so small you can barely see
It reaches out to touch the blue
The only one to watch is me.

Its leaves, like lacy curtains, droop
To hide the ancient scars of growing well
Birds still nest, though time is drawing near
None can know the stories this tree could tell.

Dramatic yellow/green leaves in spring
Preclude the start of nature's changing scene
Now stands the willow in all its glory
As nature turns the other leaves to green.

Its branches flow in downward sweep
Trunk stretching, reaching for the sky
Leaves hang down so close to water and
This tree in turn will someday fall and die.

Something more will call to us
Nature's ways are known to few
A tree may die, but seeds are sown
We are the same; enjoy the view.

July 7, 2020

One By One - It's Fall

The lake, North Bay, like glass reflects it all
A mirror imitates life and the fall
So quiet, smooth, tempts me to walk upon.
A stately maple all dressed up for fall
Disrobes her leaves one by one till naked
She stands for winter's inspection and rakéd
Leaves have lost their lovely wine-red glow
And soon become a carpet for the show
Then decay for food and another day.
Idyllic scene is smashed, a gang of geese
Noisily invade, shatter my glass lake
Into a million ripples that they make.
    On the grass, eating like tomorrow will not come.
    Red and gold leaves lose their color one by one.

October 30, 2020

The River

Our lifetime is a river
Events unfold by its shore
It flows from birth to death
There is an end, there is more.

From tiny tributaries
From drops to a river grand
It lives for a vital purpose
Brings life and death and land.

Water nourishes the earth
Flora, fauna and man
Starts with just a trickle
Ends with a sigh in sand.

We drink a glass as life begins
Through promise and birth as we call
We toast the new, dismiss the old
Make our way through rapids and falls.

Our birthright is told as a story
From the starboard to the lee
If you read the signs carefully
You'll see that the river is me.

There are many diversions
From the river to the sea
Take the left one or the right one
But keep the center free.

We lift our glass as life extends
We wonder what the fee
We know of course that life will end
But the river, forever, is free.

July 25, 2020

Boathouse

The view from the boathouse is wild and free
At sunrise deserted, the lake and the trees
Early fisherman, a day on his boat
Cuts through the blue with his message of hope
Seen from the rooftop, far end of the lake
Its cedar planked sides give a rustic strife
The beach at its side stands ready for life
Early attendants set boats on the sand
Waiting for people - to give them a hand
Kayaks and sailboats, canoes, take your choice
Then out on the lake just using your voice
Telling the sailboats to learn how to tack
    I'm telling you guys, here's what you lack
    The ability to sail and bring the boat back.

July 27, 2020

Detritus

Lazy, hazy summer morn
The winds dance, the clouds play
Sun ray breaks through, soon is gone
Light summer rain has come to stay.

Seagulls aloft float on the wind
Whitecaps break on the rocky shore
Shells move up and down with the tide
I watch, I believe that nature has more

To teach us than that huge floating crate
With boxes of nothing from far, far away
Or a million gallons of oil as a slick
Don't let the children go out to play.

The winds come swiftly, trees start to sway
High top grasses whip as they sigh
Nature might deal a blow on this day
Nothing compared to the fuel from the sky.

The day grows darker, thunder is heard
Lightning is striking the land and the sea
The rain is torrential, the sand starts to move
Get ready to run and head to the lee.

The storm is immense, but soon passes by
Some things are changed, not the earth or the sky
A storm just cleanses, then leaves on the scene
Detritus and trash from ships passing by.

July 27, 2020

Nature Vs Man

The trees in spring are lovely things
I hate to see them lose their leaves
But summer comes and winter goes
What wonders Mother Nature weaves.

Again in spring the leaves appear
They look so grand each spring
Each season has its mortality
And in his time man thinks he's king.

The trees and leaves will outlive man
If he doesn't destroy them first
We need houses, roads and buildings
Man will never quench that thirst.

So close each season, let it go
We know the seasons have no fear
That man is king means not a thing
With each season, we hope we're here.

November, 2020

None Can Ever Win

I woke up early morning and was pleased
The fall had turned to winter and the freeze
Had turned North Bay into a silver mirror
Reflecting trees so stark, there was no shore.
Almost seemed like nature made an error
Nature makes no error, only weather.
Leaves of sleeping trees become regatta
And then a lifting wind tilts up their sails
And off they go, warping around the track
Like racing leaves they know cannot come back.
The wind whips high, crashing to the shore
Those leaves will not return again before
    But some continue racing with the wind
    In a race they know, none can ever win.

December 4, 2020

An Ending

A whispering jet scars the sea blue sky
Like a very small bird seen from afar
The welts start to heal as the jet flies by
Nature's providence, the sky does not scar.

Not so the earth, we trample and tear
The bulldozers scratch, the oil rigs skewer
Animals disperse, the forests do shiver
Alas and alack, our earth is a sewer.

Shore to shore plastics afloat in our seas
Garbage forever, it does not degrade
Seabirds and fish see it as a lure
They swallow it down, life starts to fade.

All of our efforts to keep our lives safe
From terrorists' bombs, thieves on the run
None of it counts, it's this hard to say
The poisons we plant will mark life as done.

Remember the days when earth was so green
Then steel blue oceans became garbage bins
The odors may get you before plastics do
The world and you will answer for our sins.

We may have time before the planet goes gray
The bulldozers scratch, the oil rigs skewer
Time will not linger, the hours and the days
Approach ever faster, our earth is a sewer.

Listen well, my people of earth,
Hear this message I'm sending
If you don't change your ways
And clean up this mess
Then for Earth there will be
    An ending.

January 2019

CHAPTER 5

MISCELLANEOUS POEMS

*D*o you like your poetry obfuscated by torturous Sisyphean vocabulary? Do you like it convoluted by turgid and enigmatic verbiage? Do you like arcane, esoteric abstractions? Do you like references in verse to medieval madrigals you've never heard, or to ancient mythological lore?

Well, you won't find any of that in Ed Schwartz's poetry. His poems go straight from his heart to your heart.

The following is a collection of poems that are neither about nature nor about love. Some take you back in history, one on a magic carpet ride. Some are about aging; several are whimsical; others philosophical.

And some just plain funny. Enjoy!

Wind And Tides

A ship becalmed, anchored here
The sun sinks low upon the sea
No wind, no waves, no breath of air
A seagull hovers to the lee.

A storied ship, its tales untold
The hold is filled with silks and grains
Has come from lands beyond our ken
Will leave again and nought remains.

This ship's endured some mighty storms
The planks and sails show signs of stress
The masts are straight, the ropes are bowed
They've all seen waves that never crest.

She sits here now, in quiet dignity
A rest for all, but the crew can't hide
The wind returns and stirs the sails
The captain's off with the morning tide.

Where she comes from, where she goes
On land our footprints leave a trail
But on the sea there are no tracks
Come dawn, ship's gone, a trace of sail.

October 22, 2020

Lesson Learned?

Do you believe the world will change from Covid?
You'll never shake a hand or use less gas
Little has changed since the time of poet Ovid
The plague of black held the world in its grasp
The flu made many people take their final gasps
Again it changed little as everybody rasped
How can this be, we knew so much, much too fast
Did the rich man give his money to the poor?
Kings and queens and senators all stepped down?
And everyone decides they'd like to work from home?
Now who's the one that's thinking like a clown
The world will change in increments, it's said
    But people won't, the masks will soon come off
    And we'll end the Covid crisis with a cough.

May 25, 2020

Abolish The Seasons

I listen to the silence of winter
I see the first flowers, touches of spring
Then comes the sun, the heat of the summer
And relief of what a cool autumn may bring.

Snow is beautiful, covers many mistakes
Spring is lovely but it also brings storms
Some summers, so hot, they melt all the norms
Some autumns pretend that winter is not born.

Winter can be hellish, sub-zero and frost
Spring is for lovers, I feel for their loss
In summer, so hot, the heat is the boss
In autumn, a bad year, leaves all of us cross.

What can we do, the year is just fleeting
We'll ask the President for a meeting
Then ask the Congress to abolish the seasons
We, like Congress, no rhymes and no reasons.

November 28, 2020

In The Eye Of The Beholder

You see the things that I do
But in very different ways
You see the sea at sunset
I see the end of days.

You see the ocean languid
Dark clouds begin to form
The beach is yet your playground
Before the coming storm.

A painting by Picasso
Some laugh, where is the head
But I see striking moments
And a palette of yellow and red.

The music of the masters
Lays down a tender thread
I listen to the radio
Masters are lucky they're dead.

We celebrate our victories
Now I know I'm getting older
Victory for one, defeat for another
It's all in the eye of the beholder.

June, 2019

Compromise

Where are the men of yesterday
Where have the statesmen gone
Relearn the lost art of compromise
Between king and queen and pawn.

How did we ever get to this point
What have we learned from lore
Where do we go if we fight every word
If you read history, this has happened before.

All the knights and ladies of Congress
Who will rise on this new found day
They must listen to other voices
They cannot have it one way.

Be you right or left, we must not fail
At end of term, majority will tell
What goes around comes around
And you'll find that payback is hell.

If half the votes are against
Then the other half must share
Or all will go down in chaos
You must listen and try to be fair.

So compromise, compromise
Then bring the world to light
Minority becomes majority
No one is always right.

What is wrong with compromise?
What is discussion for?
If we can't talk brother to brother
What next? Do we go to war?

Look at the failing economies
Around the world and then
Reclaim the art of compromise
Let's not go through this again.

December, 2018

Tear Down The Past

Universities don't teach anymore
There's parties, drinking and drugs
And when they do, one point of view
Our students are becoming thugs.

Open our borders, let all come in?
Tear down the statues, erase the old men?
Change our history, don't let them look back
It's happened before, it will happen again.

Rewrite the books, all our heroes will fall
Capitalism down, the gap Socialism fills
Pay my tuition, income for all
Who pays the bills ... you will.

Our founding fathers were not perfect men
Some even owned slaves, does this change the fact?
They lived in a time much different from ours
They birthed our country through compromise and tact.

Don't take religion and God from our lives
Your words are no better than those of the past
In one hundred years they may look at your life
Words you utter now may make you outcast.

So live your life, listen to both sides
You may not agree but you'll find in the end
We must all be one country, let Democracy rule
Compromise a little and cultivate new friends.

December, 2019

The Glass Wall

I am separate from people
I feel it each day
I am not like them
What can I say.

I don't feel things
I see from afar
There's a glass wall around me
I'm alone in a bar.

I say I have loved
Had to learn what that meant
I married, had kids,
My wife heaven sent.

I learned that love
Is an acquired taste
If you work with each other
And don't argue in haste.

I'm still outside
After all those years
But I've trained myself
To live with my peers.

It's a lonely life
With no one to hold
Just try to fit in
Don't stay out in the cold.

So please learn to give
Accept joy in return
It will lead you to love
Or thoughtful concern.

March, 2018

Politically Correct

Shall I stay, shall I go
It tumbles through my mind
Yesterday I was here, today
It seems another time.

People talked, they'd say good day
They meant it with a smile
Today's not safe, hold your tongue
I'll be gone in just a while.'

There was a time, I'd speak my mind
And others listened too
Not so today, it's gone away
We must not think, as others do.

Those vaunted Halls of Ivy
We learned to think and reach
The basis of Democracy
For all, freedom of speech.

Not mine, not yours, but all of us
We could say what came to mind
Knowledge and search for liberty
It's going away, there's no more time.

If invited to speak on campus
An honor you duly accept
Make sure your subject toes the line
Or you won't be politically correct.

May, 2016

The Rain Is My Tears

When she first came
Sparkle in her eyes
The sun in her smile
The need in her cries.

When she was two
She learned to say dad
The roses in her smile
I was glad to be dad.

Her first day at school
A hot sunny day
The smile on her face
Said she's ready to play.

My little girl
She grew up so fast
One day daddy's girl
Next, part of the past.

But that's how it goes
And that's how she grows.
She walked on her stage
And played many roles.

Then life stepped in
Love at its best
Two boys and a girl
God's gift was a test.

She was diagnosed
When the last child was born
The sparkle in her eyes
How soon it was gone.

On a cold rainy day
They buried my fears
All color was gone
The rain is my tears.

But our life must go on
Her daughter in my lap
I miss my daughter's smile
Her daughter makes me laugh.

She had a sparkle in her eyes
That belied her youthful years
Love does not die easily
And the rain is my tears.

November, 2019

One Small Light

A light flickers on, a baby awakes
It senses at once that liquid is life
Cries for its suckle, the magic it makes
Father who's working, a sibling that's bored
Then life steps in for this gift from the Lord.
He's given a name, his story is stored
Childhood to teen and college years, beyond
A mate and a child, new light flickers on.
A light flickers off, his mother is gone
Father's not well, soon he's head of the clan
As time flies by, love, what makes the man?
Struggling to figure, what was God's plan?
    Live your life, you'll never know what it's about
    The end comes to all — a light flickers out.

September 9, 2020

I Am But A Man

1959

This is me
This is who I am
I stand at your side
I am but a man

I see myself
I live inside this frame
Sometimes soil, sometimes sand
I am but a man.

When I was young
I did not know
What was inside me
When will I grow.

Will I make music
Will I have a child
Much less a woman
Will I just go wild.

What is my depth
Where will I land
Where will life take me
I am but a man

2019

This is me

I know who I am
I still stand at your side
I am but a man

I see inside this
Gaunt thin frame
Husband, Father, Grandfather
At my age some pain.

As I grew older
I found my way
Love and hard work
What more can I say.

I made my music
Did I have a plan?
No, life works that out
I am but a man.

I wrote my poetry
Not known through the land
But that was not the point
I am just that man.

Old days new days
My life is grand
My grandkids read my poems
I was nothing until

I became that man.

January 2019

The Twisted Road

What twisted roads
Our eyes perceive
When thinking of
The lives we lead.

We never know
From step to step
Which way to turn
Is it correct?

Every turn you make
As you look back
Could lead you wrong
And that's a fact.

Nobody leads
You decide
Only in you
Your mind resides.

The road so twisted
Your mind's in the way
The fates decide
And you cannot stay.

As you grow old
As days do fade
You shouldn't regret
The steps you made.

There is no past
No going back
Turn left or right
There is no lack

Of people who will
Take wrong turns
Then blame it on fate
From them you must learn.

You are the one
That took this road
And nobody else
Can break that code.

July 1, 2020

Faithless Youth

How faithless youth can be like blowing sand
Joyous meanderings on lovely untouched skin
That vibrates at the slightest touch of hand
And then flies off to reach another land
Leaves him flailing, and wonders where she went
Realized late, she was not what heaven sent
I hope I never was that young at night
I never saw that this was worth delight
The love that I could see and want that time
Was never anything I saw or felt or might.
Take heed you adolescent little prince
And speak the words that make her heart fly high
    Free that little tremble in her coquetry
    Just memorize a few lines of poetry.

July 1, 2020

God Is Time

What is God, where is He, a child may ask
You cannot see Him, you answer, much too fast
He knows everything and is always aware
If you're happy or sad or in great despair
He knows all because He is part of you
He sees through your eyes, He knows you are fine
Because your God gives you nothing ... but time
Created in His image, because He is us
Hears your prayers, no answer, and thus
Time answers your prayers as you adjust
God gives people life, what's life if not time
Your body and mind must have maintenance
It comes not from God but by using good sense
Your guide to your time is happiness
To waste time is hell, spend it wisely, that's best
If you use your time wisely, life is well spent
    I know that many won't believe this rhyme
      But from what I've known and heard ... God is Time.

October 30, 2020

Witless

The moving hand writes, having writ moves on
But does it know that it is half of half
What it has writ is known as lively wit
But does it know that people stop and laugh
And seeing where its burning candles lit
At both ends and doesn't know the laugh of it
The hand is writing as its way of giving
Because, God knows, it has to make a living
Puts to parchment words people need to hear
Though these words drive people to depression
To you I will give this one concession
You'll find the written word has more to fear
    Than moving hand who thinks it's a Wilde wit
    This lonely hand doesn't know the half of It.

June 24, 2020

I Am

I am the dark and I am the deep
I am the one who lets you sleep
I am the one that no one can know
I am the sun and I am the snow
I am the one, to all of you pray
Time is foretold, not one more day
I am the one to whom you confess
It matters not, wear shroud or dress
I am the one you hold in your hand
I am the one who in time makes you sand
I am the place where everyone goes
No heaven or hell, it's all just a pose
    Sleep well, my people, for tonight I may be
    Coming for you through eternity.

May 18, 2020

I Want To Own My Life

They said my life is all cut out for me
What I would be is known to only me
My life involved with freedom that I see
To let my mind resolve in its own way
The way to go and leaving fear aside
Shall I become an architect today
A poet or a congressman with pride?
Won't you leave me, please, to choose my way
You think you know me better when you say
But your old way of thinking has me down
It's time for me to strike off on my own
And reap the rewards that I have newly sown,
    And maybe sit right down and write that poem
    With all that education? This may be my home.

October 19, 2020

Mistakes Happen

All people are products of their mistakes
Each mistake affects your life - like a quake
That rattles the earth, leaves it be, but changed
Some mistakes may hurt but most rearrange
You cannot know what makes you as you are
But use each one to help you raise that bar
You are the product of your family tree
And all your history points to what you'll be
A trembling hand can make a stronger mind
A deafened ear may help you hear a rhyme
A sloppy word may galvanize your speech
And with your good voice give you greater reach.
    Prior faults are sad, if you let them be
    Use your head and heart, mistakes can set you free.

September 27, 2020

How To Write A Sonnet

1. Who thinks a sonnet is easy to write?   10
2. A dunce does not know when the fruit is ripe   10
3. A poet though will wander through this way   10
4. And takes a line, something he feels, to say   10
5. Ten syllables per line, count, one to ten   10
6. Make no mistakes, professor counts them all   10
7. If you do miss a count your grade will fall   10
8. Your teacher is immune to his mistakes   10
9. Ask him, be assured, you will get no breaks.   10
10. Now fourteen lines is max in a sonnet   10
11. More than that your class will ride you on it   10
12. Recite to the class your vapid comet   10
13. If you still think sonnets easy to write   10
14. Stand before class, don't count, to their delight.   10

September 5, 2020

My Grandfather

Home I remember like will-o-the-wisp
So far back in time, the floors were swept dirt
My feet never clean, my hands and my fist
New country, we come, with a clean blue shirt
The floors were all wood, with a table and chairs
Wherever I walk, I see homes filled with stuff
People unhappy 'cause they don't have enough
My house is a palace, don't have a lot
But job, free country, my back may be sore
I do love to work, it gives me a cause
To learn what I like and what to live for
A wife someday, maybe children, I pause
    To mark how far I have traveled alone
    To finally come to that place called home.

July 10, 2020

The Common Man

A school teacher, lawyer, a deacon's son
Adams could never have dreamed in his time
Received at the Court of Versailles as one
Of common men who stepped up to the line.
Washington was an officer of men who
Volunteered to fight; they followed a man
Who would fight British taxes to the end.
There were common men in Congress, who gave
Of their time, though our army was mired in sand.
Names not known today, many buried in our land
Were not revolutionaries but soldiers …
For cause. Liberty, God, home was their plan.
    Defeating a vibrant British Army that way
    Common men became a force none could stay.

August 14, 2020

Ode To The Country Peddler

Crusty old peddler, his pack on his back
Treks through the wilderness, village to town
His beard is in tatters, his hat is a wreck
The day has been long, his face wears a frown
Now where will I rest, here under the stars?
No farm in sight, maybe under that tree
Slip off my pack and build a small fire
Twelve miles today, I am more than just tired.
A little dry meat and a hot cup of tea
Our country was started by traders like me
Expected am I, where my customers wait
A few more sales and I'll have a clean slate.
    For this is the way that my story began.
    Remember my work and learn from my plan.

August 1, 2020

Bread And Salt

Our guests arrived late last night
With apologies, they were not at fault
We showed them their rooms at even-time
And gave to them some bread and salt.

It is tradition in many climes
Friend or foe, lame or halt
We give freely to those who come
Guests will be welcomed with bread and salt.

If your pride is hospitality or
A new home built upon the hill
Leave a plate of the "good bread"
Along with salt and good will.

Bread is a symbol of unity and good
When welcoming an unknown crest
Salt is a symbol of prosperity and
Security for a foreign guest.

Eating bread and salt with another
Is considered a moral obligation
"There is bread and salt between us"
The start of a new tradition.

In England they have tea and crumpets
Sometimes a little of the brew
Hospitality born of tradition
And getting together with you.

In the U.S. you must serve some coffee
And maybe a bagel and cheese
And sometimes, sir, you must have a beer
A burger, a hot dog - but cease.

Tonight we will have a memorial
And toast to our friends who are dead
Then leave for their ghosts who remember
The tradition of the salt and the bread.

June, 2019

Dragon Boy

I am a boy
I have a wagon
What I really want
Is my own dragon

To play with me
And fly me there
Wherever I want
Through the air.

What do dragons eat?
People, I guess
I'll teach him to stop
That silliness

He'll stay in my room
No, better a cave
If Mom finds out
My goodness, she'd rave.

Get it out of my sight!
But Mom, he is mine
Dad gave him to me
And I don't have much time.

I must teach him to eat
The things that I bring
And not bother the postman,
A leash made of string.

Then at the parade
I'll fly him right by
My friends are amazed
As I zoom through the sky.

But the mayor and elders
Took one look at him
Get him out of town
Or we won't let you in.

When Daddy came home,
Did you bring my dragon?
Sorry, said Dad
Your wagon's your dragon.

We'll paint it tomorrow
Put on wings and a head.
That sounds pretty good
Let's do it, I said.

June 11, 2020

Shining Armor

Oh come my friends and see this simple knight
Who comes to Locksley, no servant at his side
He sets his sword so he won't have to use it
For this old knight does not want to fight.
The knight relies confidently on his wit
Because the poor man has to take a shit
No opener of cans within his sight
Just peals of laughter from those few men nearby
Our simple knight might just sit down and cry
When a large and sad old beggar passed him by
"Two pence, good sir, if you could only try
To open up this butt box with this pry."
    "A beggar, sir, you need a finer man, or four."
    The poor knight's shining armor shines no more.

May 14, 2020

A Magic Kind Of Travel

In the magic carpet showroom
New models have just arrived
Come on into Omar's
You're going for a drive.

In the luxurious Sahara
We have this brand new thing
Just fantastic for the desert
Called air conditioning.

If you're going for a long drive
Say from Cairo to Loch Ness
Make sure your carpet has the best
You won't go wrong with GPS.

For general entertainment
Or the music of the spheres
We have a brand new Bluetooth
Put these buds into your ears.

If your carpet gets musty
From sand, rain and mist
Bring it in, we'll make it clean
With our own brand Magi-Kist.

So hurry in to Omar's
We don't have many more
To build a rug with all these knots
All our fingers are getting sore.

If you don't believe in magic
Or a flying carpet for cash
Please don't take this test drive
You must believe or crash.

July 17, 2013

This Old League

We're much too old
To feel this damned young
Our ages are just numbers
And we're still having fun.

Here comes a strike
A spare or a blow
Or by god a railroad
We never can know.

Some days bowl good
Some days bowl bad
They all become average
For these moms and dads.

We start out slowly
Our bones need some oil
Nothing comes easy
We spin or we spoil.

They say we are old
Nothing comes to mind
Except one of our youngsters
Is just ninety-nine.

Don't worry about old
It gets us all some day
Become a bowler, Hi Roller
Let your worries roll away.

You ask what place our
Team came in last fall?
It doesn't matter as long as
We're in any place at all.

It's time for our banquet
Not peaches and honey
Just bring on the food
And give us our money.

This old league keeps on rolling
Each week our way we wend
Say hello to your teammates,
     Good neighbors, good bowlers,
          Good friends.

May 2019

Good News - Bad News

Two old buddies, ninety plus
Sitting in their rocking chairs
The sun is shining, the air is warm
Do you remember the World's Fair?

Right here in Chicago
Great White Way at night
Merchandise from everywhere
Introducing electric light.

Cost a dollar to get in
Lines awaitin' everywhere
The world did come to see
People walked around and stared.

But that was so long ago
Such fun our time has been
Yeah, bottom of the ninth
One hit the Cubbies win.

When did they win the series?
I think it was nineteen - o - seven
Yeah. You got the date right
But, is baseball played in heaven?

What brought that on, Joe
We still have years to go.
Jim, if you get there before me
Would you somehow let me know?

That night his buddy passed
He heard a whisper in his ear
Hey Joe, I got to heaven
And they do have baseball here.

Then there is baseball in heaven
So everything is right
So, Jim says, That's the good news
But the bad news, is...
    You're pitching tonight.

July, 2020

Heaven Or Not

My neighbor, ninety-four, "My head's in a whirl.
What in the world is happening to the world?"
My offhand reply put a smile on her face.
"Maybe," I said, "It is the end of time,"
As I fiddled with my glasses and wine.
"Maybe," she said, "I'll get to that heavenly place.
Do you believe in heaven, my friend?
If you don't, where do you think you will end?"
I had not given much thought to my grave
Or to heaven or hell, I'm not that brave.
Just find me a plot of land when I go
Let me sleep deeply, say good night, I'm down low.
    If you get to heaven, drink from that cup
      Won't you please tap me on the shoulder and
               Wake me up.

December, 2020

Hands

You had no say when mom and dad
Brought you screaming into the world
There was no sudden flash of light
As your own little world unfurled.
You had no say, but as you grew
Your time would come to make your mark
That is, my boy, if you really knew
That life would never be a lark.

Your parents signed their wedding vows
Soon you clung to your father's finger
And so we sealed the bargain now
As the pride of man does linger.
We sign on now that we will love
Our wives, our children, our sacred vows
Until the end when we rise above
Then sealed with the slightest bow.

My father's touch was rough and hard
My mother's soft as a dove
Father taught me how to work
Mother taught me how to love.
The differences between the two
Were miles apart, but similar
The harder hand taught manly ways
The softer more familiar.

The first time father shook my hand

He said, "You got it right in one,"
Was the day I felt my bargain made
Between a father and a son.
He stood there like an old oak tree
And I a seedling in his shade.
My sister's hands, I barely knew
From birth to death her days were few.

We don't shake hands, the guys and I
An older man, a teacher, yes; high fives O.K.
A slap on the back, a punch and a cry
Learning and playing, having fun today
Listen in school, well, try anyway.
Some facts come through, some do not stay
First grade to eighth, a waste of time
Then high school and the long, long climb.

Welcome to my class, the man was tall
He crushed my hand and I felt small.
"That's not a shake of hands," he said,
"Grasp my hand and squeeze it tight.
The mark of a bargain, I teach you to write."
I thought of my Gramps, dying in bed,
He shook hands "Goodbye, live in my stead."
I never lost sight of the bargains I made.

Bumped into a girl I knew in school
Knocked over her books, felt like a fool
Got down to help her, discovered her hand
Found I was touching a brand new land.
Holding hands, innocent, the first time you feel
It holds within a promise, time will reveal
No shaking of hands, this feeling was real
Young as we were, we tried to conceal.

Shake hands with the boss and the office crew
A bargain inferred, you do what you do
You signed on the line, the bill's coming due
A house and a wife, a baby, no clue.
Still the bargain stays on, you and your ways
Do the best that you can for the rest of your days.
That baby will soon grab your thumb so tight
Welding your hearts together for life.

Decades have passed, your children are grown
They made their own bargains, their families they own
Your mate has departed and you're all alone
Eighty-five is old, how much more can there be?
Two months go by and you seek history
You talk to old friends of arthritis and food
You want something more, but what is the good
The country closed down and you understood.

But life is resilient, I met someone who
I could talk to of music and books that we knew.
She was an artist and I liked to write
We talked and we talked for hours, how grand
Then one day I said, "Mary,
        Are we too old to hold hands?"
She reached for my hand, put both around mine,
Said "I wanted you to say that for a long, long time.."

Our hands now are clasped for as long as we can
And I say to you all
        "You are never too old to hold hands."

January 6, 2021

Lightning Source UK Ltd.
Milton Keynes UK
UKHW011850010721
386496UK00007B/408/J